Table of Contents

How to Read Auras

A Complete Guide to Aura Reading and Aura Cleansing

by Yuna Willows

Introduction

There's an old saying that goes: "People have eyes, yet they do not see." This is true in many ways. In the natural world, particularly, it refers to the constantly changing and evolving energies that are present everywhere yet most people are not aware of. These energies, also called bioelectric fields, are more commonly known as auras.

In Greek, the word aura means "breath of air." It's this air that envelopes the bodies of many living things. It's this breath of air that can strengthen or weaken a part of something, depending on the kind of aura.

Auras, simply put, are the colored halos that are emitted and carried by all living things in the world. The nature of the aura will represent certain aspects of a living thing including but not limited to:

- State of mind

- Health

- Personality

- Mood

To clarify, auras differ from chakras. Albeit related, chakras are an entirely different concept. Chakras have a more rooted characteristic, and refer largely to the central aspects of a person's being. The aura refers to the halo or energy that can be seen around a person. It is this halo, the aura, that you're going to learn how to read.

Those who can see auras are presumed to have very sharp senses and further honed them specifically for the task. This is why most people need to learn how to actually see these energies. What's interesting to note, however, is that many people unknowingly encounter these energies in their daily lives. As you read through this guide, try to be aware of these encounters to help familiarize you with the experience of aura-reading. This will make for more graphic and easier learning.

Learning how to see and interpret auras is a very useful and beneficial skill. Those who can see auras are able to:

- Understand the personality of a person better
- Unlock or advance the potentials of their own traits or talents
- Diagnose illnesses
- Improve the potency of physical and mental healing or recovery
- Channel feelings or moods to their advantage, given certain environments and people

Taking time to learn how to do this properly will positively impact much of your personal awareness and well-being as well as improve your relations with people.

Here you will learn how to sense, see, and—to some extent—use auras to your advantage and for the benefit of others. This guide will take you from the basic steps to the more advanced ones, including:

- Understanding the auras and what they look like

- Knowing your current capacity to see them

- How to properly sense and see them

- Exercises to help you see auras

- Interpreting auras

- Manipulating these auras

Much of these concepts will be better understood through practice rather than through reading. Still, understanding what exactly it is that you're doing is the essential first step. Keep this in mind as you go further into the guide so you do not end up reading past any chapter sooner than you should. Like everything else, practice makes perfect.

Chapter 1: Understanding Auras

Visualizing is half the battle. Auras are not one of those "you'll know it when you see it" things. In fact, many people live their lives seeing auras without even knowing it. That's why you need to know what they look like.

The "halo" description is a pretty good place to start. You have probably already glimpsed these energies at some point in your life. These experiences will be the places where you can work on your exercises because these are where the auras will be stronger and possibly more visible.

"How Do I Know if I Can See Them?"

Some people have already experienced seeing strange colors around other people and things as children. If you vividly remember some of those experiences in your younger years, then you've seen what auras look like.

Children are known to be able to naturally see these energies. You've probably heard about how a young child cries for no apparent reason when someone comes close to them. They cry because they don't like the color of that person's aura. The people around them don't understand why because they don't see the auras themselves.

What usually happens is, as they grow older, children who can see auras tend to lose focus of these things until they stop seeing them altogether.

However, the deterioration of this ability to "see" did not make those auras disappear. They're still there, and the most common of daily life experiences prove that they are. Here are some of the most common instances where you make use of or interact with auras even without your knowledge:

- You can guess what kind of person somebody is even before you talk to him or her.

- Even if you can't explain it, you have a hunch that a person is lying or hiding something.

- You can "feel" that someone is watching or staring at you, or you can tell that someone is in another room or on the other side of a wall.

- Some people make you feel happy or uncomfortable, even when they're not doing anything. In some cases, you don't even have to be aware that they're there.

If you can relate to any of the above instances, then you've "felt" auras, and being aware of these feelings alone can be very beneficial. You will learn that you can do so much more when you know how to see, interpret, and even control them.

So if you've seen auras before, or you're aware of the presence of these auras, you're already steps ahead. If not, don't worry. It doesn't mean that you can't learn to see these auras; you just need to practice a bit more.

"What Do They Look Like?"

Auras are still part of a person's essence—they are not magic. Therefore, they have a physical aspect.

Auras around people are composed of both electromagnetic (EM) and infrared (IR) radiation waves with varying frequencies. The high-frequency ultraviolet (UV) light reflects most of our conscious actions such as our thoughts, actions, and feelings, and is generally easier to spot with the naked eye.

Auras generally have an oval shape and envelope the person. They extend slightly above the person's head and below the feet, going into the ground. The egg-like shape will usually extend up to two to three feet away from the person emitting the aura.

Having various frequencies, the aura will also have multiple levels. There are seven levels in total, with each emanating from different chakras and having different frequencies. Every layer also provides different kinds of information, and the strength and size of the energies are affected by different factors. These levels are, however, in one way or another, interrelated.

- **Physical Level.** This is the base level, where your body is. It requires mere physical comfort and pleasure. It's not strictly considered a layer since it is the actual human body and not an aura in and of itself.

- **Etheric Level.** This is the aura that vibrates closest to the body and reflects physical health. The aura can be as far as two inches from the body and presents as a blue color. It is the indicator of whether or not a person is feeling pain or pleasure.

- **Emotional Level.** This goes up to three inches from the body. Because emotions can be so volatile, this part of the aura is often observed to have rainbow colors and will look muddied up when a person is feeling negative emotions. People who are observed to have problems with this layer will feel certain problems in the etheric and mental layers as well.

- **Mental Level.** The mental aura extends between three to eight inches from the body and has a bright yellow color. It reflects the person's thoughts and ideas.

- **Astral Level.** This is the spiritual level of the aura and emits bright rainbow colors when a person's spiritual health is strong. It extends about one foot from the person's body.

- **Second Etheric Level.** This is a negative space that contains all the blueprints of the physical realm. The color will usually vary and extends two feet from the body.

- **Celestial Level.** This is also a spiritual level of the aura, but it has a different function. This is where most communication with the spiritual world takes place. It also indicates high levels of spiritual feelings. It comes in various bright pastel colors, extending up to two and a half feet.

- **Ketheric Level.** This layer goes beyond three feet and is manifested in threads of a golden color. This is the level that represents most of your life's experiences as well as your relationship with Divine beings.

It will take practice to be able to identify and distinguish these layers from one another. Auras will always vary, but given time and practice, the descriptions above should give you a pretty good idea about how to tell which is which.

Chapter 2: Seeing Auras

The human eye has a naturally limited view of frequencies: somewhere between 0.3 and 0.7 micrometers. In the color spectrum, that would be violet to red. In most instances, these colors can be perceived properly only with the use of certain tools, such as spectrometers. This is because our eyes, through the process called resonance, can only see three photosensitive cells, namely red, green, and blue. Hence, we have the RGB concept of color.

Our eyes are pretty much just scratching the surface when it comes to auras which involve a much more complex set of light vibrations.

Training Your Eyes

Learning how to see auras, therefore, will require two things. First, it needs great effort to make one's eyes more sensitive to the subtle variations of color. Secondly, it requires an expansion of the perceivable range, one that goes beyond visible light. This can be done with the following:

- **Peripheral Vision.** Years of watching television or staring at the screens of smart phones and computers have made the center the most utilized portion of our eyes. This means two things: Firstly, the central part of our eyes is the most worn out. Secondly, that some parts of the eye have been trained to function in ways that may not be consistent with seeing auras. This is also another reason why children, in their young age, can see auras more easily.

While the parts of our eyes that correspond with our peripheral vision may be dormant, they are potentially ideal for watching auras.

- **Increasing Exposure.** The human eye, as the old saying goes, functions much like a camera and thus requires stronger concentration in order to be able to see less visible traces of aura. As a roll of film requires more exposure in order to clearly capture dark scenes or images, so does the eye. Our eyes are more accustomed and trained to catch quick movements. However, seeing an aura requires focus on one area or object for long periods of time, so that the eye can get used to being exposed to what an aura looks like.

These two methods are combined into concentration exercises that will train the left and right hemispheres of the brain in order to enhance the communication between these two. There are many different kinds of exercises that can be used, but one thing they all have in common is that they aim to help you practice focusing on a certain object in order to give your peripheral vision the chance to pick up subtle vibrations.

These exercises usually involve staring at an image for short periods of time. Do them on a regular basis and make sure to focus. More often than not, it's more effective to successfully focus on the given image for uninterrupted short periods of time than to devote longer periods of time but only briefly glance at the image. Try to focus for as long as you can, and then stop once your concentration breaks. That way, you can develop a minimum period of focus and just work your way up.

Training with images, however, will never be enough. Make sure you switch between the concentration exercises and a real person. After all, that's where you'll be seeing auras from.

Attempting to See the Aura of a Person

Start with a person set up before a white background. The background has to be plain white because colored ones will cause auras to appear as different colors. Without proper knowledge of color combinations, you'll end up misinterpreting the auras you might see.

Once the subject person is settled, start focusing on one aspect of his or her face. For beginners, the best place to start is the center of the person's forehead. This particular point has been observed to be a rich source of auric presence, because that's where one of the chakra points—the third eye—is found. This is why in India, people put a spot called a *bindi* on their forehead—it's considered to be an invitation to see one's aura.

Start looking and focusing on the spot for 30 to 60 seconds. The length of time you spend practicing to focus will eventually increase as days go by and you get more and more used to these exercises. Once you reach the 30 or 60 second mark, begin sensing things within your peripheral vision. If you've done your exercises correctly, you'll be able to properly observe your periphery without taking your eyes off the center.

Once you've gotten a good look at the aura, you'll want to have a more permanent impression of it in your mind. To do this, close your eyes. For about two seconds you'll see only the aura. In this phase, timing is key to perceiving the aura perfectly.

Looking at Your Own Aura vs. Other People's

You can also practice observing your own aura. Find a softly illuminated room with a white background you can place yourself in front of. Stand in front of a mirror at a distance of about 1.5 meters. Do the same thing as you would with another person.

Keep in mind how more effective it is to practice on another person. This is because you will most likely be looking at other people anyway, and secondly, you'll be able to see the aura of other chakras like the throat and the heart, which is slightly harder to do when staring at yourself in a mirror.

Tips:

- Practice makes perfect. Make sure you do these exercises diligently for at least ten to fifteen minutes per day.

- Having problems focusing? Try meditating before you begin the exercises. While it may seem like the mind-clearing aspect of meditation contrasts the goal of gaining focus, it really doesn't. Rather, it complements the exercises, because you get to clear your mind first and condition your body to perceiving auras through the proper mantra.

- Don't be discouraged when you don't see an aura immediately. Nobody gets it right the first time. You might also want to double-check if you've set up your exercises right (i.e. if you've used the proper background).

- Try not to bother with interpreting what you see yet. You can work on that in the next chapter once you get the hang of spotting the aura.

- It might also help if you get expert training from those who can see auras already. A couple of training courses won't hurt and may be the just help you need.

Chapter 3: Interpreting Auras

Once you've learned to perceive auras and see them clearly, the next step is to know how to interpret what they mean.

Filtering A Person's True Character

It's a well known fact that personalities are not always consistent. There are different factors that affect a person's current mood and behavior. The purest form of a person's character is known as his or her "True Nature." To illustrate, a person's nature is his or her being excluding all the mannerisms, stereotypes, and other superficial actions.

This is exactly what the aura represents. By simply looking at the aura of a person, you get to understand a person's true nature without bothering with the facade. This is also how you can spot a person who is lying.

Basic Rules in Interpreting Colors

There are a host of interpretations for auras. These depend on where it is found and what state it is in. More advanced interpretations also include factoring in surrounding circumstances to allow you to better understand what exactly the person is feeling (i.e. if you detect an aura of joy, you can tell what exactly a person is happy about). Here are some basic things to keep in mind when reading auras:

- Brighter and more colorful auras entail a stronger and healthier spirituality. This means that whatever aspect of a person that aura pertains to is in an optimal state. Conversely, darker and fainter looking auras mean there might be a problem in that area.

- Distribution of the aura is indicative of balance and health. A person with a more dispersed or uneven aura may be unwell in some way. People with evenly distributed auras obviously have better control of themselves. With the help of technology, the aura can also be used to detect certain illnesses.

- There are "clean" and "dirty" colors. Clean colors are bright, monochromatic, and shiny. They usually denote something positive. Dirty colors, on the other hand, are smoky and denote something negative.

- A change in the color of the aura obviously entails a change of circumstances. Sudden spikes in the aura around a person's head normally indicate a sudden change of thought.

- Be mindful of auric pairs. Colors in the real world will normally express a specific colored aura, which is its pair. The pairs are:

  o Red and turquoise

  o Orange and blue

o Yellow and violet

o Green and pink

These pairs work alternately (i.e. orange colors in the real world show blue auras while blue colors show orange). This is important because it will keep you from getting tricked into thinking that you're looking at a certain type of aura. For example, a man wearing a yellow shirt might look like he's giving off a violet aura when in fact what you're seeing is the shirt's own aura.

Common Color Interpretations

The meaning of a color will not always be constant, but these ones, although primarily tested on the head part of a person, sum up the general rules quite well:

- Blue is the color of expression. It's the color that signifies the transfer of knowledge or the understanding of it. People teaching or giving lectures will usually give off a strong blue color, while students who are learning something will give off a light blue aura.

- Red is the color of passion and strength. This can be either a good or bad thing, depending on how strong the color is. In some cases, a really strong red color can be a sign of selfishness, although at times it can be seen as a strong will.

- Yellow is all about the person's state of optimism. Weak yellow auras often indicate frustration or anxiety, while stronger ones show confidence and intelligence. You can tell if a person is nervous or not by looking at their yellow aura.

- Orange indicates health and energy. Strong orange auras can be good or bad since they either indicate high levels of ambition or high levels of selfishness. Creativity can also sometimes be measured with this aura.

- Green connotes healing; it also measures one's capacity to share love and affection.

- Shades of indigo and violet connote spirituality. Violet auras show how spiritually strong a person is, while those with indigo auras are in a state of spiritual learning.

- Black indicates some kind of damage.

- White indicates purity.

Take note, however, that some say that white can also be a sign of illness, since it represents the absence of harmony among the colors. In fact, it has been observed that an aura turns white a couple of hours before someone dies. This is why some cultures use white as a symbol of death.

Chapter 4: Common Auric Obstructions

Folks who have learned how to read and interpret auras will eventually want to know how to improve auras through various procedures or therapy. Obviously, people will want to remedy and achieve better auras and avoid negative auras.

While learning how to enhance auras is essentially an entire different course of training altogether, knowing some basic concepts will allow you to avoid problems relating to auras.

Prevention: What Creates Negative Auras

Generally, negative thoughts meddle negatively with the aura. These negative thoughts or blockages come in many forms. Among the blockages are:

- Spiritual toxins

- Negative energies

- Psychic attacks

- Personal negative experiences

- Distorted auras or auras with holes either personally emitted or channeled towards the person

Again, the things above can manifest in many forms, but it needs to be stressed is that these blockages are not all strictly supernatural. These blockages can also come in the form of sickness, physical pain, or weakness as much as they can be about mental or psychological stress. This is why auras can be a way to determine the overall health of a person.

While there are some instances where blockages are deliberately caused by other people for whatever reasons, they don't form part of the common scenario. More often than not, people's auras are affected by more common day-to-day problems.

Effects of a Negative Aura

The short answer is: they're not good for you, or anyone else. What they actually do is make things worse for people. This, of course, is relative. For instance, a person who is of good health and strong personality, when blocked with negative aura, will only feel less energetic or productive, and it will seem as if there's nothing wrong with them to the naked eye.

For people who are already sick or have naturally problematic personalities, it will manifest in a worse way. They will need to have their auras cleansed or enhanced for their well-being fairly regularly to compensate for this.

A very practical way of telling if someone is suffering from negative aura is by looking at how they relate with others. It could be that because they're so fatigued from the aura, they don't feel as approachable or appear as nice. People will also feel somewhat disconnected from their spirituality or from nature itself. And of course, they are also more likely to get sick.

Cleansing Your Aura

An aura becomes healthier when a person collects positive energy to himself or herself. People often make the mistake of assuming the process is very complex and difficult, but cleansing one's aura is basically about being good to yourself and, consequentially, your aura.

- **Meditation.** Balance is an indicator of healthy aura, and meditation is one way to maintain this balance. Taking the time to use mantras to focus your personal short and long term goals can give your aura a good boost.

- **Cleaning your body with water.** This is probably the cleansing method that's most taken for granted. When bathing, take time to smoothly comb your hair with your hands and run your hands down your body. Alternatively, you can also take time to get soaked in the rain.

- **Exercise and play.** Remember what happens to the boy who is all work and no play? Your aura gets dull when you're too stressed. Take time to go out, enjoy the breeze and the sunshine, and have fun.

- **Try these add-ons.** There are some things that have been associated with good aura. For example, whisking feathers in a sweeping motion on your body can help improve the aura. Smoke from lavender, sweet grass, and other herbs can either be breathed in or simply applied on the body. Soaking in saltwater is said to be beneficial for the aura as well.

Try to look up other ways to cleanse the aura. There are so many ways to do this, with methods varying greatly between cultures.

Chapter 5: Auras and the Environment

Because your aura partly reflects your relationship with your environment, it doesn't hurt to try and fit in with your surroundings or, if the environment is within your control, make it fit you. The goal is to make your aura in tune with the world around you.

This is not something new. Many cultures have employed guidelines in interior decorating and dressing that are in tune with their beliefs. Although these practices are not purely based on color, those that deal with color largely use the concept of making auric color match with the environment.

Strong Points and Auric Pairs

Before moving on, you'll want to be able to identify your **strong points**. These are what ideally should be in tune with the environment. Look at your aura a couple of times (you should be able to do this after the practicing the previously discussed exercises), and take note of your most dominant aura. That's your strong point.

With that, just keep in mind the auric pairs discussed earlier. These pairs and the strong points will be your guide to matching your aura with your immediate environment.

How to Match Auras

Redecorate your home. The good thing about with auric color pairs is that they work with most interior décor themes. So whether your home is oriental, rustic, minimalist, or modern, you can still effectively match auric colors without affecting the central theme of your home. To do this, just include the color that pairs with your aura keeping with the motif of your home décor.

Be careful, however, not to overdo it. If your aura is green, don't turn everything in your house pink. For one thing, it's going to cause a terrible imbalance. Secondly, it's just tacky.

Harmonize with the environment. Of course, you can't possibly redecorate every place you are in. The best thing to do in this instance is to adapt and adjust yourself. If the aura where you are doesn't match yours, find nearby places that match yours the closest. When you travel, you can also bring certain objects with you that match your aura, so you'll always be in your zone. Take note that your clothes can also be part of your environment, so wearing bright colors that match your aura can do wonders as well. These are obviously more feasible adjustments compared to redecorating a place that's strange to you.

Avoid dull colors. They tend to neutralize bio-energies rather than just harmonize them. They do nothing to your auric pairs, much less help improve your state of being.

Avoid negative people. They're part of your environment, too. Obviously negative people are easy to spot, but there are also people who appear to be nice and agreeable who actually possess negative auras. Your training in seeing other people's auras, however, will help you avoid these "seemingly" positive people as well.

However, it is important to remember that nothing is ever set in stone. Auras and personalities change. It doesn't mean that you should not be friendly to people with negative auras, or that you shouldn't go to places that don't match your color. In the end, see how the situation affects your overall mood, because that's ultimately the end goal of improving your aura.

Conclusion

In a world where knowledge is power, knowing how to see, interpret, and improve auras can be particularly beneficial to your daily life. Knowing how to strengthen auras will allow you to manipulate them to your advantage.

Take note that the world's best leaders and the most charismatic people have been known to have strong auras, whether they themselves were aware of it or not. Learning auras can also unlock doors to other arts that you might find interest in, such as astral projections and healing.

Know that this guide does not cover everything you need to know in order to master the art of reading and enhancing your aura and that of others. People who practice this art as a career or passion will often branch out to specializations, and it will take lots of time and dedication to be able to master them.

Rest assured, however, that absorbing this guide will give you a good start at reading auras, whether you're planning on just learning the basics or building up for a more specialized course. This kind of knowledge is a big step toward making life work for you in every way.

For now, take the time to review the basic concepts whenever you can and continue to practice. At the very least, your new found knowledge of auras will help you become healthier and happier with your life.

Finally, I'd like to thank you for purchasing this book! If you enjoyed it or found it helpful, I'd greatly appreciate it if you'd take a moment to leave a review on Amazon. Thank you!